Recollections
 of
 World War II
 in
 Poetry

Bernard Surgil

Recollections
of
World War 11
in
Poetry

Bernard Surgil

Copyright © 2014

All Rights Reserved

No portion of this publication may be reproduced, stored in any electronic system, or transmitted in any form or by any means, electronic, mechanical, photocopy, recording, or otherwise, without written permission from the author. Brief quotations may be used in literary reviews

ISBN: 978-1-4951-1992-7

Cover photograph: Getty Images

First Printing – October 2014
Second Printing - September 2015

Library of Congress Control Number: 2014914130

Printed in the United States by
Morris Publishing®
3212 East Highway 30
Kearney, NE 68847
1-800-650-7888
www.morrispublishing.com

Foreword

We are caught in a tide of tales here, stories that include moments of panic, bursts of valor, endurance, pain, victory. What better form to record these intimate yet universal emotions than the vehicle of poetry, with its heightened consciousness and wisdom born of time.

In this collection, Bernard has safeguarded and presented a period of time when war seemed honorable and men felt privileged to serve their country.

In the voice of his 19-year-old self, soldier in the 2nd World War, Bernard conveys all of the emotions overwhelming him in his unique experience, ones that marked him, formed him and changed him. Now in his 89th year, his memory as keen as his skill for recording it, he gives us a stunning experience to re-live through his eyes.

Truth and clarity are the keynotes of his memories; Poetry is his gift to soften the sharp edge of reality. Combined in this way, Bernard has given us an unprecedented insight of an era we often prefer to erase from our memories. Remembering is his way of insuring against further war-born atrocities. "There should be nothing here I don't remember."

It has been my sincere pleasure to mentor Bernard in this poetic presentation. The stories tell themselves but the form helps the reader see this not only as history but as a personal memoir stamped on the soul of the writer and indelibly changing the awareness of the reader.

This is a bookshelf treasure.

Dorothea Bisbas
Poet Laureate, Rancho Mirage, California

Prologue

By assembling my experiences in The Philippines during World War II, I aspire to a time and place when America was engaged in a righteous war.

To articulate how an east-coast-urban, eighteen year old college sophomore thought and felt evolving from a civilian-soldier, innocent in the ways of war, to a combat-veteran wiser in the ways of the world.

What he learns about war, what war has to teach, how war corrupts. How the madness and vagaries of war befall combatants, local citizenry, and the countryside when nations wage war no matter how noble the cause.

Finally, by creating this collection of recollections, I wish to leave my children and grandchildren, a brief history of my life and times before they were born.

Although humanity has written about war since the beginning, each generation is obligated to warn succeeding generations about its follies. Unfortunately, Homo sapiens DNA continually reject the idea.

Herewith is my contribution to the cause of peace.

Bernard Surgil [1925 -
Rancho Mirage, California

Acknowledgements

To Poet Laureate, Dorothea Bisbas, whose vision, insight and encouragement turned a collection of memories into a book of poetry. Who for the past four years has mentored me in the art of poetry, expanded my poetic education, and honed my poetic skills. I hope I continue to make her proud.

To Linda Silverberg, whose creative cover design captures the essence of my poem; whose computer expertise assembled this book into a publishable format; whose love and devotion turned my eighth decade into the best decade of my life; for letting me know I can always count on her support and encouragement no matter the enterprise I undertake.

To Anita Harmon, your editing skills helped turn many a confused phrase into an enlightened line of poetry, your suggested enjambments always clarified the "sense of place," your questioning why, when, where, constantly made me rethink which words to choose.

To Wednesday's Rancho Mirage master's poetry class, who continually offer me an amazing array of ideas, perspectives and possibilities. Thank you for your ongoing support.

For

Linda
Jaime
John
Rita
Steven
Dale
Jesse
Sabrina
Halle

**Leyte Island
Philippine Islands
October 20, 1944**

There should be nothing here I don't remember
                                      Richard Blanco

Deafening salvos startle
scarlet flashes follow
midnight sky blazes
        gun powder pollutes
                putrid smoke chokes

A somber chaplain paces the deck
Soldier would you like to pray?
an atheist   I stay silent
                morning light outlines
                              an island in flames

Overhead missiles whistle
shock-waves swiftly follow
awe resolves to reflection
            it's my nineteenth October
                        will there be more?

Time to disembark
I straddle the ship-railing
grasp the cargo netting
        hemp rungs sting my fingers
            hemp rungs sag beneath my boots

Once the LST fills   like a pelican bursting
free of the sea   we lunge towards Leyte
silently I do my drill
    reach the beach   find a dune
      aim   shoot   advance   repeat

Crouched against the hull   violent vibrations
shudder craft to a halt   *We've struck a freakin'
reef*   coxswain yells   *Abandon ship*
    loaded with gear   a very deep breath
      I jump boots first into Leyte Gulf

There should be nothing here I don't remember

Plummeting like a stone   I discard gear
loath to see belongings disappear
as unlaced boots fall away
      lungs on empty
        scream oxygen

Surfacing aside a floating body   mouth
nose   ears clogged with gasoline traced
salt-water   I swim toward Palo beach
    waterlogged fatigues
      sap my strength

Not sure I have enough left   I throw caution
aside when a gasoline drum floats by   shrapnel
strike?   despite risk   I hold on
      drill kicks-in
        reach the beach

2

Japanese artillery   relentless   spray the shore line
the waters beyond   U.S. battleships retaliate   the
sky fills with missiles   detonations pound
                        shockwaves pummel
                                    mayhem prevails

Relieved bare feet finally feel sand
I wade to shore   collapse at the tide-line
momentarily rest   refocus   find new gear
                       amid deafening explosions
                                  bullets everywhere

    There should be nothing here I don't remember

In oil-stained   sand-caked   soggy fatigues   I
slither along the beach   reach a GI behind a dune
find he's dead   shot through the head
                        like a trapped deer
                               I momentarily freeze

Eager to crawl away   find another sandbank
a hail of bullets forces me back   resigned
I lie aside the dead GI   squeamish
                       sick to my stomach
                            mouth full of bile

Sun   temporarily comforts   until a stench
unlike anything smelled before induces gagging
forces me to spit up
               death's reek
                    war's stink

Despite my haze   I retrieve his carbine
his helmet   undo his backpack   freeing his
web-belt accidentally rolls him face-up
                 his eyes   open
                           turn mine away

I glance at his boots   ambivalent   I unlace them
slip my bare feet into where his once fit
is donning a dead man's gear desecration?
                      civilian me   guilty
                         soldier me   expediency

As shouts of medic compete with cacophony
pinned behind a dune   aside a body reeking
death   anxiety turns to anguish to prayer
              Grandpa in heaven   please save me
                  I don't want to die like this

When he appears   haloed in soft amber light
calmness descends   until aircraft from sinking
carrier   "USS Princeton"   breaks the trance
       [atheistic me astonished
                  child-like language surprises]

With GI's scattered amid the sand   planes   with
no place to land   join the fray   strafe   break the
impasse   flying on empty   they crash atop trees
                      two survive
                         rest of squadron dies

    There should be nothing here we ever forget

Leyte Island   The Philippines
October - December   1944

Over deep rutted dirt roads
past bleak fields   through ravaged
villages   liberators   bestowed with
flowers   press on   hamlet to hamlet

dispensing cigarettes   C-rations
candy   to a barefoot populous   who
sits on its haunches   cooks over wood
eats with its fingers   smells from smoke

Men   mostly brown-skinned   use
water buffalos to plow   use fingers
to plant   use scythes to harvest rice
in paddies flooded knee high

Women   regal postured   water
bearers since childhood   child
bearers by middle teens   assume
responsibility for familial needs

Palm-thatched wood frame houses
built on stilts   room for monsoons
recycle waste thru a hole in the floor
to squabbling pigs   cackling chickens

Population   mainly Roman Catholic
largely devout   adorn their local
parishes with heavenly riches
despite being earthly poor

When we reach Tacloban   Leyte's
capitol   church steeple   peopled
with Japanese snipers   compels
we shell   toppling spire

Citizenry   where it can assist
name Japanese hiding places
take local collaborators to task
we take the city street by street

Courthouse   jailhouse   riddled
a pagoda   hostel   in flames
Philippine National Bank
vault wide open

Mid-November   monsoons arrive
foxholes fill   attempts to bail   fail
my survivor's creed   *"If you treat rain
like air you'll be unaware it's there"*

Mid-December   sisters of misery
my malaria   a typhoon   one minute
burning hot   another freezing cold
continually   sopping wet

Granted leave to attend to my needs
I hike untold miles in a wind driven
typhoon when my Jeep gets stuck
in hubcap deep mud

Christmas Eve   1944
Leyte Island
The Philippines

In need of malaria medication   I wend my way
from the front to the X on my map   a church
converted to an army field hospital

topped with tarps   band-aides to bandage the
downed steeple   collapsed roof   target for
typhoon swirling winds   torrents of torrential rain

"Doc won't do rounds till mornin"   drawls a
medic   *"Swallow this   Find a cot   God-damn
church is friggin wet"*

Too weary to contest   too wet to care   I locate
a cot   await the kick quinine transmits   to quell
chills   induce sleep

Raindrops splatter
                Church-bells chime
                              Choir a cappella
Dismaying?
              Dreaming?
                            Delirious?

            I prop myself up

a young padre   dressed in cassock black
stands under an umbrella   sing-songs
morning prayers

a boys choir   attired in robes barely hiding
their muddied toes   render in Tagalog
"Christ is born let us adore him"

Latin liturgical words   castrato-sounding lyrics
despite red-hot fever   debilitating chills   I'm
reminded of home

**The South China Sea
January   1945**

Two weeks away from the front
time it took to repress my malaria
time it takes to liberate Leyte
time it will take to mop-up
stragglers   die-hards

I rejoin my outfit
aboard a troopship
headed for Luzon
ready to participate
in another invasion

Using sun's warmth
to regain strength
west winds
to clear my head
I reflect
stumbling ashore
in oil-stained
sand-caked
soggy fatigues
teenage
civilian-soldier
Leyte
October   20
1944

Today
battle tested
leading by example
a soldier's soldier

Destination Cabanatuan
January – April   1945
Luzon Island
The Philippines

As breeze differs
from whirlwind
rain from typhoon
to surprisingly light
resistance   landing
on Lingayen Gulf
Luzon
differs from landing
at Palo Beach
Leyte
as punch differs
from knockout

Once ashore
headed east
on terrain
flat to hilly
we battle
to Cabanatuan
a city infamous
for its prisoner
of war camps

The closer we come
fiercer the resistance

At the Cagayan River
we try   for five days
suffer heavy losses
to dislodge enemy forces
attempting to forge
the swollen river

Day six
reconnaissance radios

"We're not taking fire
Japs have abandoned site
We're crossing   over and out"

"Red" and I
Luzon Island
The Philippines

Once we hear the Cagayan
is safe   "Red" and I agree
after months without a bath
this may be our only chance

We walk to the bank to bathe
a soft pop   followed by a loud
swoosh   "Red"   suddenly pitches
forward   face profiled on the grass

Astonished to see a flare
embedded in his back   I
instantly realize   incendiary
blue-white phosphorous
is too hot to extract

"Medic!   Medic!"

Smell of burning flesh
grows stronger   I watch
helpless as "Red's" hapless
form slowly burns to death

By the time assistance arrives
"Red's" insides are ashes   while
the medic blankets what remains

I walk to the river   bathe   amazed
how unfazed I seemingly seem

Nightly   "Red"   visits my sleep
we replay the scene   we walk
side by side   we're inches apart
suddenly disaster strikes   I awake
wet with sweat

Beyond Cabanatuan
May - August   1945
Luzon Island
The Philippines

Once Cabanatuan is liberated
we pursue the Japanese into
the Sierra Madre Mountains
in terrain so tortuous   enemy
snipers slow pursuit to a crawl

Mortar rounds
lobbed from on high
create massive land slides
obliterate our trail

Months on end
intense daytime heat
high humidity   nights
when temperatures drop
bone chilling cold
we slog over rugged terrain
in unforgiving conditions
to a broad plateau
designated   Base 2

C-47's parachute-drop
water
C-rations
ammunition

August 1st

Army Headquarters
Cabanatuan
via shortwave radio

*"Re-enforcements being dispatched
to bring Company back to combat strength"*

Eager to determine when
I accidentally pick-up an Australian
ham radio station playing American
jazz   wistful   I tune in when I can

**Base 2   August 1945
Luzon Island   The Philippines**

[**Via shortwave radio   Australia**]

*"August 6th   The United States
dropped an atomic bomb on Hiroshima"*

*"August 9th
The United States
dropped an atomic bomb on Nagasaki"*

*"August 15th
The Emperor of Japan
surrenders   World War 2 is over"*

V-J-Day

"Advance Australia Fair"
"God Save The Queen"
"Star Spangled Banner"

Thoughts drift to home   I'm high
low   jig-saw puzzle scattered across
the globe   my books   my room
my parents   my sisters   a hot bath
college   fitting-back-in

been so long   touched   held
embraced   kissed   atop these
god forsaken mountains   I turn
giddy thinking romance

31

To war:
a Rorschach blotch
of booby-traps
sniper nests
silhouettes

To peace:
a valedictorian salute

Physically:
fighting fit
when malaria
doesn't persist

Emotionally:
never lost my way

August 20th

Army Headquarters
via shortwave radio

"Return to Cabanatuan"

It takes a week to break camp
descend the mountains

Short Lived Reprieve
Luzon Island   The Philippines

Cabanatuan rest camp
tents   cots   hot meals
primitive showers
tented latrines
5-star dream

Orderly   *"Captain wants to see you"*

*"Sergeant   orders from headquarters
We're to return to Base 2
disarm the Japanese army"*

[We just left that god-forsaken place]

*"They want a liaison to establish
contact with the Japanese General Staff
I'm appointing you liaison   You leave
tomorrow at sunrise   By the way
I'm promoting you to staff sergeant"*

[I can't believe what I'm hearing]

"One more thing"   pointing to a red spot
on his map   *"Five miles north of Base 2
there's a fork in the trail   a Jap will meet
you there   escort you to their camp"*

[You gotta be kidding]

*"Once there   tell them to run a telephone
line to the fork in the trail   we'll splice
lines   advise them the number of soldiers
to dispatch each day"*

He lights a cigarette

*"Our job will be to disarm the bastards
before they march themselves down
to trucks waiting to take them
to prisoner-of-war camps"*

[I bet the Captain got the assignment
freaked out   dumped it on me   guilt
prompted him to promote me to staff]

**Returning to Base 2
Luzon Island
The Philippines**

Day 1

During the drive
to the Sierra Madre Mountains
I observe   freshly plowed fields
children   strolling to school
roadside shops   newly stocked
far cry from earlier in the year

Against this pastoral scene
sculptures to the god of war
charred remains   trucks
tanks   an airplane

When I enter the mountains
birds chirp   monkeys chatter
huge bushy tailed rats   wild
turkeys   quails   scatter
at the sound of my boots

Perched atop the tallest trees
vultures   with giant black eyes
blood red craws   massive wings
tightly tucked against protruding
ribs   patiently wait

As afternoon fades   I locate
a clearing   set-up camp   fearing
hostile Japanese   forego fire
down a cold C-ration   stretch
out   gaze at emerging stars

Day 2

Morning
I continue the ascent   aware
as drop-offs grow steeper
a misstep   a slip means a fall
to where no one will see me
hear me   except vultures

Just before dusk   I sight a cave
cautiously enter   see animal scat
nonetheless   camp for the night

When an unidentifiable growl
disturbs the darkness   I awake
on low-alert

Day 3

Dawn
determined to arrive
at the X on my map
I'm dismayed when I do
there's no escort in view

[Is it wise to continue alone?]

when I see a Japanese soldier
run toward me   abruptly stop
bow   signal   "follow me"

Guardedly   I do

Like a draft of wind
douses a candle
the moment
my presence
is perceived
conversation
from thousands
of Japanese
stops

The sudden
stillness
shocks me
defiant stares
freeze me
force me
to dig deep
remember

[we won the war
these soldiers
are our prisoners]

will I regain my poise
aggressively wade
into the multitude
relieved they step aside
form an aisle

As I pass thru
their ranks
inadvertently
brushing
shoulders
with many
who wear
distain
as an epaulette
my escort
opens the flap
on a large white tent
signals
"enter"

General Yamashita & Me
September 1945
Luzon Island   The Philippines

I enter the tent   Japan's military
seated   stare straight ahead
refuse to acknowledge my presence

Ignoring the slight   I approach the officer
with the most gold braid   snap to military
attention   salute   no response

Heart   breathe race   brain calculates
defuse the hostility   fulfill the mission
sullenness builds   pressure mounts
desperate   I shout   *"Anyone speak English?"*

My words   like a shroud   settle on everything
around   silence   unspeakable loud   envelops
me   anxiety escalates   finally   *"I do"*   breaks
the tension   free to be   I boldly proclaim

"On behalf of The United States Army
I am here to arrange the disarmament
of Japan's Armed Forces on Luzon"

Stillness again descends until the officer
with the most gold braid   claps   signaling
the "I-do" officer   stand by my side
receive what-to-say directions

*"General Yamashita would like to hear
the orders you carry"*

*"You're to lay a phone line to the x
on my map   We'll splice-in   Begin
measures to disarm your army"*

"Are there other instructions?"

*"None for now   by the way   where
did you learn to speak English?"*

"The University of Chicago"

[Never expected to hear that]

"Excuse me my General has something to say"

Seconds later

"You are invited to join him in a modest supper"

[Rather not but best be diplomatic]

"Please tell the General   I accept"

*"The General would like to know
how can you build roads so quickly?
Keep them open   no matter the weather"*

[Nothing here I can't divulge]

"*Bulldozers and American know-how*"

"*The General would like to know
if Al Capone still runs Chicago?*"

[After all these years of waging war
this is on the General's mind?]

"*I think Capone is still in jail*"

"*General Yamashita would like to know
have you ever met President Roosevelt?*"

[What an ego   I must be important
Why else would the army send me]

"*I never met President Roosevelt*"

Satisfied with what I have to say
the General claps

Orderlies appear
as do plates   chopsticks
warm sake   bamboo containers
filled with white rice   dark greens
served family style

[How do I appear polite   yet not partake]

47

From my backpack   I offer the General
a spaghetti and meatball C-ration   join
him with another

With chopsticks   he tastes   breaks into
a broad smile seemingly enjoying
supper in a can

*"General Yamashita would like to know
is this an officer ration?"*

*"Please tell the General this ration is issued
to all Army personnel regardless of rank"*

Later   the translating officer
*"General Yamashita welcomes you
to spend the night in this tent"*

[It's dark   staying over makes sense]

"Please tell the General   I accept"

At sunrise   when the General appears
I hand him a "bacon 'n eggs" C-ration

The translator *"General Yamashita would
like to present you with a present"*

The General hands me a piece of folded silk

I come to military attention   salute   leave

48

When I unfold my gift
I'm shocked to see   hand-painted scenes
of men   women   large dogs interacting
in explicit sex acts

[What a weird thing to give someone you
just met   Why would the General do that?]

Later   I recall reading   When Samurai
warriors engage a worthy adversary
they often exchange erotica

Is this the General's message?
Was it meant for me?
or America's mighty military?

[On February 23 1946   a United States
Military Tribunal finds General Yamashita
guilty of crimes against humanity and hangs
him in a military prison in Manila]

I feel no emotion when I hear the news

The Mission
September 1945 - February 1946
Luzon Island   The Philippines

High in the Sierra Madre Mountains
on a mesa designated Base 2   98 GI's
will disarm   130,000 Japanese soldiers
      two FBI Agents will look to arrest
           a pair of notorious war criminals

Sunrise   for the next six months Japanese
soldiers will appear at the perimeter of Base 2
ceremoniously face east   ritualistically kneel
      pray to Emperor Hirohito   rise
           march single-file to surrender

Disarmed prisoners   stripped of war mementos
samurai swords   rising-sun flags   will march
themselves down the mountains to trucks
      waiting to take them
           to prisoner-of-war camps

Monies   Japanese soldiers looted from Philippine
banks   English pounds   French francs   Dutch
guilders   Philippine-American banknotes
      will overflow
           improvised containers

Two FBI agents   will station themselves
on the perimeter of Base 2   scrutinize
everyone passing through in search of
                    a Japanese national
                            his Eurasian wife

"What crimes did they commit?"

"We're not at liberty to say"

"How will you find them among
all these soldiers and refugees?"

*"We're FBI   we weren't sent
here to return empty handed"*

The FBI

November
afternoon
a crowd of civilians
dirty   disheveled
attired in tatters
appear amid
a contingent
of walking
wounded
Japanese
soldiers

Like a tiger
on a hunt
an Agent bounds
into the multitude
separates a man
from the swarm
orders him *"Stand
against the tree"*

Seconds later
his partner confronts
an Eurasian woman
orders her   *"Sit
on the ground   back
to the man standing
against the tree"*

Agents
from their
respective sites
initiate a sequence
of intense interrogations

First to break
is the woman
who bursts
into tears
acknowledges
she's the wife
of the man
standing
against the tree

Agents
swiftly
handcuff
the pair

Appearances aside
these are no ordinary
refugees

The woman
despite attempts
to look unkempt
is a femme fatale

The man's eyes
exhibit rage
being betrayed

With prisoners
in tandem
the quartet leaves

Once they reach
Manila   the couple
will stand trial
for war-crimes
against humanity

I never learn
the crimes
they committed
or their fate

The Ongoing Surrender

December
early morning
Japanese soldiers
waiting to be disarmed
push a countryman
to the ground
repeatedly
strike him
with rifle
butts

Ordered
"Stop"

They do

Whereupon
the downed
man murmurs

"Thank you   Sir"

"What did you just say?"

"Thank you   Sir"

Incredulous

"Who are you?"

*"A civilian doctor
forcibly conscripted
by Japan's military
when they retreated
from Manila"*

"Why were you beaten?"

*"At my age
I am unable to march
in a manner respectful
to the Emperor"*

"What's your name?"

"Ito Cho"

"How old are you"

"Fifty"

*"Where did you learn
to speak English?"*

*"Graduated from UCLA
lived in LA"*

*"Doctor Cho
you are now my interpreter
in a medical emergency
Base 2 physician"*

"By the way
always keep me in your sight
Some GI's feel we're still at war"

January
a Japanese soldier
refusing to accept
Japan lost the war
tosses two hand grenades
into a tent of sleeping GI's

"Medic! Medic! Men down!"

By the time Doctor Cho and I arrive
Company medic Charlie frantically tries
to prevent six G.I.'s from bleeding to death

By the light of kerosene lanterns
Doctor Cho takes command
administers morphine
removes shrapnel
deftly stitches
skillfully bandages
thoughtfully advises

"Their survival depends on blood transfusions"

Radioing Headquarters
I relate details
request transportation

Dawn
stretcher-bearers
break-neck speed
record-setting time
carry the wounded
down the mountains
to waiting ambulances

All survive the descent

By late February
I reluctantly tell Doctor Cho

*"It's time   the final prisoner
contingent will leave in the morning
There's no way you can remain with me"*

I light a cigarette
offer one to Doctor Cho
we inhale   stare at one another

*"I'm going to miss our time
together Doctor Cho"*

*"So will I my friend
Don't be troubled
I knew this day
would come"*

Concerned about Doctor Cho's
ongoing safety   I hand him a letter

*To American Commissioned
and Non Commissioned Officers*

*Doctor Ito Cho's heroic actions saved
the lives of six severely wounded GI's
when a crazed Japanese soldier tossed
hand grenades into their tent   Please
treat the Doctor accordingly*

Years later

I receive a letter
post-marked
Osaka   Japan

Dear Friend

*I wish to thank you for continuing
to save my life even when you weren't
there to do so in person   Your letter
afforded me humane treatment during
my entire internment   At my age   I
never would have survived if I were
treated as an ordinary prisoner-of-war
I am eternally grateful*

Sincerely   Ito Cho

A few years later a letter
arrives from Doctor Cho's family
telling me in part   from complications
attributable to war-time conscription
and subsequent prisoner-of-war internment
Ito died as he wished   in his sleep

Doctor Cho was 58

Mister Chang & I
March 1946
Luzon Island
The Philippines

Granted a three day pass
I covertly seek to convert
my share of commandeered cash
$ 30,000 of Philippine-American
banknotes   to United States dollars

Manila   city of bars   soldiers
sailors   marines   prostitutes
revelers everywhere   drunk

When the Chinese desk clerk
requests payment for the room
I oblige with a ten-dollar bill

 "Old Philippine money no good soldier"

"What do you mean no good?"

*"Japanese come   say Philippine money
no good   only Japanese money good
war over   US say   old Philippine money
no good   only new Philippine money good"*

*"This is the only money I have
It's late   I need a room"*

*"If I take money
maybe wait long time
maybe bank say O.K.
maybe never   understand?"*

"I do but I need a room"

"If I take money   do new rate"

"Oh!   I see   how much?"

"Fifty dollar   old money"

"Fifty dollars   that's robbery"

"No can do for less soldier"

Exasperated
I add two twenties

*"I'm hungry
is there a restaurant nearby
that accepts old money?"*

*"We have restaurant in basement
best Chinese supper in Manila
twenty dollar old money"*

Grudgingly
I hand him a twenty

Room 6
a bed   a mattress   a blanket
down the hall   a toilet   a sink

[Luxuries beyond recall]

Morning's mission
find a bank

*"We do not accept pre-war money
soldier   only U S Government issued
post-war Philippine currency"*

[What do I do now?]

when the bank manager whispers

*"I know where you can convert
your pre-war money at a discount"*

"Is the bank near?"

*"Not a bank
'Chang's Tea and Spice Emporium'
on San Francisco Street
Ask for Mister Chang
tell him Mister Alvarado sent you"*

At "Chang's Tea & Spice Emporium"
a nondescript middle-aged Chinese woman
is seated behind a counter smoking a pipe

"Mister Alvarado sent me"

I follow her
down a narrow corridor
to a beaded curtained doorway

When she steps aside
I enter a warehouse stacked
ceiling high with bales of tea
spice boxes with dizzying scents

A man in a white suit   shirt   shoes
blue tie   Panama hat   dark serious
eyes   sits in a high back chair
I assume is Mister Chang

[An Eurasian "Sidney Greenstreet"]

*"Hello   Mister Alvarado thinks
you can help me"*

In a deep calm voice
traces of an English accent

*"How much money are we discussing
soldier?"*

[Insecure over his intense scrutiny
I try to act nonchalant]

"Not a lot"

"*Young man   you know your money is worthless this is why you are here   As a private banker   I buy   lend   sell money   I cannot help you unless I know how much money you wish to exchange I wish you no harm   If you are not comfortable with me please feel free to leave*"

[Better make a deal]

"*Thirty-thousand-dollars*"

"*I will buy your money at the current rate private banks are offering   ten percent of face value*"

[Is he playing me for a fool?   No way to check him out   Find a better deal?   Maybe high-jacked   Maybe killed]

"*I'll accept your offer if you pay me in American dollars   I don't feel secure with Philippine money*"

In a tone a tad more respectful

"*I will exchange your money with fifteen-hundred American dollars and fifteen-hundred post-war Philippine pesos   This is my only offer*"

[This is almost as much as my father earns in a year]

"*I accept*"

On the way back to the rest camp

[I must devise a way to send
my mother my money]

[In 1949, The New York Times reported
The United States Government reached
agreement with the Philippine Government to
honor all Philippine American Federal Reserve
Bank Notes issued prior to December 7th, 1941
at face value]

California
April 1946

Aboard the USS Heritage
I read   rest   lose most of my money
playing craps

Dock in San Diego
bused to Camp Pendleton
soldiers who served in Philippines
automatically quarantined

Medical condition:
malaria   tapeworm   severe diarrhea
inability to gain weight   jungle rot
GI slang for tropical skin lesions

Fear truth may delay discharge

Mental state:
nightmares   screams
Medic   Medic
fire quickly spreads
never can save "Red"
creatures chase me
try to catch me
sweat awake

Fear truth may delay discharge

During routine physical

"How do you feel Sergeant?"

"Fine"

My biggest secret
I've started to stammer
wish I knew why

Testing complete
I visit the P X
find a telephone
hear the pick-up

*"It's me
I'm coming home"*

Silence
before tears